Christmas

Sarah Kelly

RED FOX

Contents

A Red Fox Book

Published by Random House Children's Books, 20 Vauxhall Bridge Road, London SW1V 2SA

A division of The Random House Group Ltd, London, Melbourne, Sydney, Auckland, Johannesburg
and agencies throughout the world

Text and illustrations copyright © 2001 Sarah Kelly

1 3 5 7 9 10 8 6 4 2

Printed in Hong Kong THE RANDOM HOUSE GROUP Limited·Reg. No. 954009

ISBN 0 09 940937 2

Introduction

What better way to make beautiful christmas objects than in mosaic? Mosaics can be made out of lots of different materials and the technique has been used for thousands of years to make pictures and patterns, and to cover treasured items. The brilliant reflective qualities of tiny pieces of coloured glass that were used on some mosaics gave a beautiful jewel-like effect to the objects that were decorated.

Christmas is the perfect time of year to use the sparkling effects of mosaic. A variety of different materials are used in this book, from sequins and glass gems to glitter and fake fur. Use as many bits and pieces as you can collect – there may already be lots of things lying around your house.

In these twelve projects you will learn how to create simple designs for christmas cards and gift tags, how to make your own baubles for the christmas tree using papier mâché bases and even how to cunningly fake a mosaic using a potato! Hopefully the ideas shown here will also give you the confidence to create your own mosaic projects.

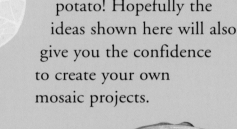

Getting started: Materials

A variety of materials are used to make the projects in this book – and most of them are SHINY! You may be able to find many things around the house, but if not, good art shops, department stores and stationers will stock the things you need. Start collecting straight away!

PAPER

- **Plain paper in bright colours** You can buy this in individual sheets or in multicoloured pads. Avoid using sugar paper, as the colours will fade.
- **Shiny foil paper** Foil that has a paper backing is much easier to stick down than ordinary kitchen foil.
- **Glossy magazines** Collect old magazines to find areas of pattern and texture.
- **Cellophane** Try to get small sheets if you can, as you only need a small amount, or use cellophane sweet wrappers.
- **Crepe paper**
- **Gift wrap** Patterned gift wrap makes mosaic pieces look more interesting.
- **Newspaper**
- **Tracing paper**
- **Clear sticky-back plastic**

CARD

Most of the projects use thin card as a base to work on. This is available from art shops in sheets or packs. If you can't get hold of card in the right colour you can always use acrylic paint or waterproof ink to colour plain white card. Don't use powder paint, as it will smudge when you stick on the paper pieces.

SEQUINS AND BUTTONS

- **Sequins** are used in lots of the projects. Look out for leaves, stars, snowflakes, crescent moons and diamonds as well as basic circles. Craft shops or department stores usually have a good selection and some may even sell bags that contain a mixture of different shapes. If you can't find the more unusual shapes, you can always cut them out of shiny paper.
- **Buttons** also look good in mosaics. Pearly white buttons can be bought quite cheaply, and you may also find some nice ones at jumble sales, markets and charity shops.

OTHER MATERIALS

- **Glass nuggets** You can buy these in candle shops.
- **Small plastic gems** Available in different shapes, these can be found in craft or bead shops.
- **Fake fur and felt**
- **Silver metallic thread** This looks lovely in the projects where things need hanging or tying.
- **Ready-mixed tile grout**
- **Small fluffy white pom poms** (like rabbits' tails) are available from craft shops.
- **Acrylic paint**
- **Glitter**

GLUE

All the projects use PVA (sometimes known as Marvin or white glue). This comes in bottles or tubs and dries clear. You will also need wallpaper paste for papier mâché.

TOOLS

- **Scissors** A pair with a good point for accurate cutting and a small pair of needlework scissors for snipping fiddly shapes.
- **Craft knife** Only use this when a grown-up is around to help.
- **Pencil**
- **Ruler**
- **Hole puncher**
- **Rubber**
- **Felt-tip pen**
- **Strong needle** for making holes
- **Small paint brush**

Getting started: Techniques

Any mosaic takes time to make, no matter how much experience you have had, but remember that the more time and effort you put into each project, the better the results will be. You may find it fiddly at first, especially if the pieces are quite small, so enlarging the designs and the pieces you use may help.

Before you start, read each project through carefully so you understand exactly what needs to be done at each stage. The projects are designed to get more challenging as you become confident with the mosaic techniques, so do some of the simpler projects at the beginning of the book before you tackle the more complicated ones at the end. New techniques are introduced project by project, but there are a few basic things that you need to think about right from the start.

DRAWING

Aways draw your outlines in pencil and remember to rub them out carefully afterwards. Don't make the line too dark and heavy. Use a light-coloured pencil if you are drawing on a dark background.

TEMPLATES

The templates at the back of the book can be used in two ways. You can photocopy them (enlarging them if you need to), cut them out and draw around them very carefully, or you can trace them. Lay a sheet of tracing paper over the template and trace the outline with a pencil. Turn the paper over, lay it on top of a spare piece of paper, and draw round the outline on this side. Turn the paper back over and trace down the design onto your card. This method makes the design come out the right way round.

CUTTING

Cut strips of paper to the width given in each project and then snip them into squares. Don't worry if the strips are not even all the way along, or the squares aren't perfect.

Instructions are given in the project if a strip needs to be cut into a special shape. Some pieces will need trimming to fit into small or unusual spaces, especially at the edges or in the middle of the mosaic. You can do this by holding a piece over the space and marking the shape that needs to be cut with a pencil. As you get more experienced you can do this by eye.

GLUING

Before you start gluing, make sure your work surface is protected with newspaper. Squeeze some glue into a saucer and paste a small amount onto each mosaic piece before sticking it onto the design. Sequins, buttons and other heavy objects will need slightly more glue. Don't overload the pieces with glue. If glue starts coming out of the sides when you press the pieces down, you are putting on too much. You'll get the best results by applying glue to each piece individually. If you find this too fiddly, try spreading some glue over a small area of the design and sticking the pieces straight onto it. The PVA has a tendency to leave a 'skin' on the spreader as you work, so keep a clean rag handy to wipe it off occasionally.

PLACING

Always lay the pieces next to each other and if you are using pieces that are all the same shape, work in lines. Leave a small gap between each piece and try to keep the gaps the same size.

RIGHT WAY

WRONG WAY

Work from the outside in on large areas, and from one side to another.

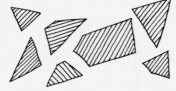

On the more complex picture mosaics, do the things at the front (foreground) first and work 'backwards' to the background.

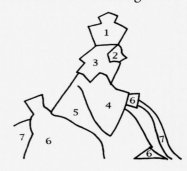

After a while, you will develop a rhythm when laying the pieces and it will get much easier. Try to keep the lines flowing, and don't be afraid to go over an outline if it looks more natural that way. All the projects will suggest a background colour for your mosaic, but when you create your own designs, make sure that the colour of the card is not the same as any of your mosaic pieces, or they will not show up. Remember, mosaics are not made by machines so they are not meant to be absolutely perfect! It doesn't matter if some pieces are a bit wonky or overlap, or if some lines aren't completely straight. All these things give your mosaics a unique charm and make them look much more authentic! The finished design doesn't have to look exactly like the one in the book to be attractive either. These projects are meant to show you some basic techniques and to inspire you. Once you've tried a few of them, you can go on to develop ideas in your own way and create your own amazing mosaics. The most important thing is to have fun.

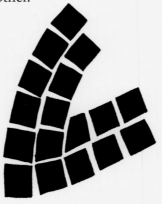

Christmas tree card

A combination of two simple shapes create this striking christmas tree design on a card.

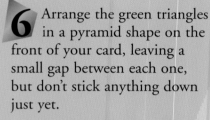

YOU WILL NEED

- **A sheet of thin black card**
- **Coloured paper in green, red and yellow**
- **Ruler**
- **Light-coloured pencil**
- **Scissors**
- **PVA glue and small plastic spreader**

1 Using the ruler and pencil, measure out a rectangle of 21 x 15 cm on the black card and cut it out.

2 With the pencil, mark the point 10.5 cm (half way) along each of the longest sides of the rectangle. Using the ruler and the blunt side of one of the scissor blades, score a line between the marks. This will make it easier to fold the card in half.

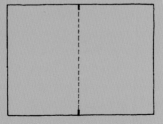

3 Fold the card in along the scored line and press it down firmly.

4 Cut a strip of green paper about 3 cm wide and snip it into triangles. You will need nine to make the tree shape. It doesn't matter if they're a bit wonky!

5 Cut a strip of red paper about 1 cm wide and snip it into squares. Again, you will need nine of these. Finally, cut out a square 1 x 1 cm from the yellow paper.

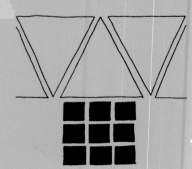

6 Arrange the green triangles in a pyramid shape on the front of your card, leaving a small gap between each one, but don't stick anything down just yet.

7 Place the nine red squares in three rows to make a bigger square underneath the bottom middle triangle.

8 Finally, place the yellow square on its point like a diamond on top of the tree.

9 When you're sure that your design looks right and is nicely placed in the centre of the card, glue each shape carefully in place.

10 You can make lots more cards using the same design. If you like, you can vary the colour of the squares at the bottom of the tree, or the background. Just make sure that the background colour is not the same as any of the colours on the tree, or they won't show up!

TIP

You can use a silver or gold pen to write your message on the inside of the card or, if you prefer, you can cut out a smaller rectangle of light coloured paper, glue it onto the inside of the card and write on that instead.

Merry Christmas and a Happy New Year

Snowflake gift wrap

A simple potato cut and some white paint are all you need to create the realistic mosaic effect of these snowflakes.

YOU WILL NEED

- **Some sheets of dark blue crepe paper, or any other thin paper**
- **White acrylic paint**
- **Small potato**
- **Sharp knife**
- **Kitchen roll**
- **Old saucer or plate**
- **Newspaper**
- **PVA glue (optional)**
- **Blue and silver glitter (optional)**

1 Ask a grown-up to help you cut a thin rectangle from a potato (as if you were making chips) about 1.5 cm wide and 1.5 cm deep. Cut off the end of the rectangle so it is square. Dry the potato cut with the kitchen roll.

2 Put lots of newspaper down to protect your work surface. Squeeze a small amount of paint into an old saucer or plate. Dip the end of the potato cut into the saucer and move the paint around with it so that the paint spreads out and covers the end evenly. Press the potato cut into a clean area of the saucer a couple of times to get rid of any excess paint.

3 Start at a top corner of the paper about 4 cm away from the edge. Make a vertical line of seven squares, leaving a small gap between each one. Then turn the potato cut so that it is facing 45 degrees from one of the corners of the middle square. Print a line of three squares up from the middle square. Repeat around the rest of the corners.

TIP
You might want to practise printing a snowflake on a spare piece of coloured paper. When you feel confident that you can make a good snowflake shape, then go on to the sheet of crepe paper.

TIP
If you dont like working in lines, you can always print the snowflakes in a random pattern.

4 Make a line of snowflakes across the sheet of paper. Try to leave an equal space between each snowflake. When you come to the edge of the paper, make another line underneath, and continue until you get to the bottom of the sheet.

5 Each potato cut is good for about two standard size sheets of wrapping paper before it stops giving sharp prints. Make another potato cut when you need to.

6 Give extra impact to your design by making the snowflakes sparkle with glitter. Mix PVA glue in with the acrylic paint and print the snowflakes as before. After completing each one, lightly sprinkle it with glitter to make it sparkle.

7 When you have finished, gently lift up your wrapping paper and shake the glitter onto another sheet of paper. Then tip the glitter back into its pot.

8 Lay each sheet of wrapping paper out flat to dry. Then use them to wrap your presents!

TIP

If you haven't got enough room to make a complete snowflake at the edge or the bottom of the page, you can either leave a gap and trim the sheet down later, or you can carry on printing, taking the incomplete design right to the edge of the page.

Snowflake gift tags

Add an extra special touch to your presents wrapped with snowflake gift wrap. These pretty tags use a mosaic of shapes cut from silver or holographic foil paper for extra sparkle.

YOU WILL NEED

- **A sheet of thin dark blue card**
- **Silver or holographic foil paper**
- **Cup**
- **Pencil**
- **Scissors**
- **Tracing paper**
- **PVA glue and small plastic spreader**
- **Hole puncher**
- **Fine silver thread**

1 Turn a cup upside down and use it as a template to draw a circle on the blue card. Draw a circle for each gift tag you want to make, then cut them out.

2 Trace the six-line star template on p. 38. Lay the tracing paper over the circle so that the middle of the star lies in the centre of the circle, then trace down the image. This will give you the basis for your snowflake design.

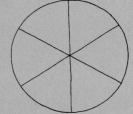

3 Cut out strips about 5 mm wide from the silver paper. Decide on one of the designs below and cut out the right number of squares, strips and triangles. Then follow the instructions for the design you have chosen.

4 When your design is finished, use a hole puncher to make a hole in the tag. Cut a length of thread about 20 cm long, fold it in half and push it half way through the hole in the tag, loop end first. Thread the remaining end through the loop and pull firmly.

5 Write your christmas message on the back, and stick the tag onto your parcel with clear sticky tape.

DESIGN ONE

You will need eighteen triangles, six squares and eighteen strips (squares cut in half) to make this snowflake.

1 Stick six triangles along the lines in the middle of the circle, with their points facing in to the centre.

2 Stick two more triangles above each of the centre ones and then stick strips between the second row of triangles to make a circle.

1 Stick two strips along each line radiating out from the centre. Position the first ones so that their bases touch. Then stick the triangles between them.

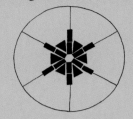

2 Stick one strip horizontally above the triangles. Then stick two strips vertically above them.

3 Stick two strips horizontally above the third row of triangles so that they meet in the middle of the triangle's base, and then stick a square above them.

2 Using four strips for each arm of the snowflake, stick them horizontally in two rows of two above the vertical strips, with their ends meeting in the middle of the line. Finally, lay a square on its point like a diamond above them.

3 Snip a corner from each of the remaining long and short strips. Do one half with the cut sloping diagonally from right to left, and the other half sloping from left to right.

DESIGN TWO

You will need six triangles, six squares and thirty-six strips (squares cut in half) to make this snowflake.

DESIGN THREE

You will need twelve triangles, thirty strips (squares cut in half) and twelve longer strips to make this snowflake.

1 Stick six triangles along the lines in the middle of the circle, with their points facing in to the centre. Then lay six more above them pointing in the other direction.

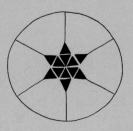

4 Stick the short strips on either side of the top vertical strip. Then stick the long ones below them, making sure the ends don't poke over the edge of the tag!

Papier mâché baubles

D ecorate papier mâché balls with foil paper, sequins or buttons to make these beautiful glittering baubles for the christmas tree.

YOU WILL NEED

- **Newspaper**
- **Wallpaper paste**
- **Plastic pot**
- **Measuring jug**
- **Teaspoon**
- **Small ball (about 7 cm across)**
- **Vaseline**
- **Craft knife**
- **Thick needle**
- **Fine silver thread**
- **Shiny foil paper in gold, silver or other bright colours**
- **Circular and star-shaped sequins in bright colours**
- **Small flat buttons in red, green or pearly white**
- **Scissors**
- **Hole puncher (optional)**
- **PVA glue and small plastic spreader**

TIP
You need to make the papier mâché balls a couple of days in advance – they need to dry out properly before you can decorate them.

1 Cover your work surface with newspaper, as making the balls is a very messy process.

2 Tear a sheet of newspaper into strips about 3 cm wide, and then tear these into small strips. You will need one sheet of newspaper to cover each ball.

3 Now mix the wallpaper paste. Measure out 150 ml of water in the measuring jug and pour it into the plastic pot. Add a teaspoon of wallpaper paste, stir it in and leave for three minutes. Then stir it again. It should be runny, but not too watery. Add more water or paste as necessary. This should be enough for about six balls, but you can store any unused paste in an airtight container.

4 Cover the surface of each ball with a layer of Vaseline. This makes it easier to remove the layers of papier mâché when they are dry.

5 Now comes the messy bit! Dip your fingers into the paste and smear it onto a strip of newspaper, then press it onto the ball. Cover the surface of the ball with one layer of paper, smoothing down the strips as you go.

6 Continue covering the ball in this way until all the paper strips have been used. Make each layer as even as possible by smoothing down the strips with your fingers.

7 Put the completed balls on a plastic bag and leave them somewhere warm to dry. Turn them occasionally so that they dry evenly.

8 When the balls are completely dry, ask a grown-up to help you remove the covering of papier mâché. Cut round the ball with a craft knife and twist off the two halves.

9 Take one of the halves and glue a small square of shiny paper on the top with PVA (choose a colour that you're going to use for the background). Pierce two small holes through the centre of the square, about 3 mm apart.

10 Cut a piece of thread about 20 cm long and push it through one hole and out of the other. Knot the ends together.

11 Rip up some small strips of newspaper. Place the two halves of the ball together (match up areas of writing or pictures so they fit together perfectly) and stick the strips of paper over the join with wallpaper paste. Leave to dry.

12 When the ball is dry, completely cover it with a layer of the shiny paper you used on the top. Cut the paper into small random shapes and stick them on with PVA, making sure no newspaper can be seen. This creates a nice shiny background that will show between the spaces of your mosaic.

13 You are now ready to decorate the baubles! Choose one or more of the ideas shown on the next page, depending on what sparkly things you have managed to collect.

SHINY PAPER – TRIANGLES

1 Cut some shiny paper into strips about 1-1.5 cm wide and then snip them into triangles (see p. 8).

2 Starting at the top, stick the triangles over the ball with PVA. Working outwards from one area at a time, stick them as close together as you can. Triangles that are too big to fit can be trimmed. Don't stick the string by mistake!

SHINY PAPER – CIRCLES

1 Use a hole puncher to make lots of circles from different coloured shiny papers and put them in a container to mix the colours up.

2 Starting at the top, stick the circles next to each other as close together as you can, picking them randomly from the container.

SHINY PAPER – SQUARES

1 This style looks a bit like a disco mirror ball! Cut some shiny paper into a wobbly strip between 5 mm and 1 cm wide and then snip it into squares. You will need the bigger squares for the middle of the bauble and the smaller squares for the top and bottom.

2 Start by sticking a ring of the biggest squares around the middle of the bauble.

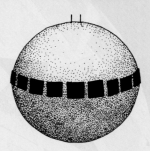

3 Work up the bauble in rings, with the squares getting smaller and smaller as you reach the top. You may have to leave bigger gaps between the squares here. Repeat on the bottom half of the bauble.

SHINY PAPER – CRAZY-PAVING

1 Cut out a small section of shiny paper and snip it into lots of random shapes (triangles, squares, rectangles and anything in between!), but don't make them bigger than about 1.5 x 1.5 cm.

2 Starting at the top, stick the pieces next to one another, as close together as you can, like a sort of mad jigsaw puzzle! Trim pieces to fit into the gaps if you need to.

BUTTONS

You can use a mixture of sizes, colours and shapes, but try and choose buttons of a similar depth so your bauble doesn't look bumpy. The buttons need to be flat and no bigger than 2-2.5 cm in diameter.

Buttons need more glue to make them stick to the bauble than the paper shapes. Work on one small area at a time, making sure it is dry before you move on to another section. Take care you don't accidentally dislodge any of the buttons while you are working. Keep gently pressing the buttons down as the glue dries and keep an eye out for any ones that slip.

TIP

If you find it too fiddly to hold the ball while you are sticking the pieces down, rest it on top of an empty jar.

SEQUINS

Sequins look terrific on these baubles, as they really sparkle in the christmas tree lights. You can use circular ones or experiment with other shapes such as stars or snowflakes. Holographic sequins look great, too. Use the same sticking technique as described in the buttons section.

Figgy pudding card

Use a crazy paving mosaic technique to make this delicious-looking figgy pudding on a square greetings card.

YOU WILL NEED

- **A sheet of dark red card**
- **Ruler**
- **Pencil**
- **Tracing paper**
- **Old glossy magazines**
- **Scissors**
- **PVA glue and a small plastic spreader**

1 Using the ruler and pencil, measure out a rectangle of 28 x 14 cm on the red card and cut it out.

2 With the pencil, mark the point 14 cm (half way) along each of the longest sides of the rectangle. Using the ruler and the blunt side of one of the scissor blades, score a line between the marks.

3 Trace down the pudding template on p. 39 onto the front of the card.

TIP
You can cut out the same colour from different magazine pictures to make your mosaic, but make sure they're not too different in shade. If your colours have some writing or a pattern on them, it will make your mosaic look more interesting.

4 Look for blocks of dark brown, creamy white, green, red and yellow in the old magazines.

5 Cut the colours into blocks or strips and then snip them into small random shapes. Cut three small circles out of the blocks of red.

6 Start the mosaic by doing the foreground areas. Stick down the three red circles for the holly berries and then do the holly leaves with the green pieces. Stick triangles into the points of the leaves and fit the rest of the pieces around them, gradually filling in the leaf shape. Trim the pieces to fit into odd gaps if you need to.

7 Next, fill in the pudding's topping with the creamy white pieces. Start on one side and work across, laying each piece next to another and trimming some to fit if necessary.

8 Do the pudding using the dark brown pieces in the same way you did for the topping.

9 Fill in the background in yellow, leaving a small gap around the edge of the card.

10 Try making another design for your next card, like the robin on p. 39, or invent one of your own.

Jewel night-light jar

A glass jar covered with glass gems is transformed into a beautiful night-light holder, which sends little jewels of coloured light around the wall when the candle is lit.

YOU WILL NEED

- **A small empty glass jar, as shallow and as wide as possible**
- **40-60 glass gems in greens and reds**
- **PVA glue and small plastic spreader**
- **Ready-mixed tile grout**
- **Newspaper**
- **Old rags**
- **Gold acrylic paint**
- **Small paintbrush**

1 Cover your work surface with newspaper. Hold the jar with your hand on the inside and cover the outside edges with a layer of PVA. Put down the jar and leave it to stand for a few minutes until it becomes tacky (when the glue starts to go transparent).

2 While you are waiting for the glue on the jar to become tacky, start to 'butter' the backs of the glass gems with a thin layer of glue.

3 When the jar has become tacky, press the gems carefully onto it. Starting at the rim (if there is one), stick on the gems as close together as possible. When you get to the end of a row, choose a gem that will fit tightly into the space that's left.

4 Hold the jar from the inside again and cover the rest of it with gems, working in vertical rows. Make sure that the gems on the bottom don't go beyond the base of the jar. Use bigger and smaller gems to fit the spaces as you need to.

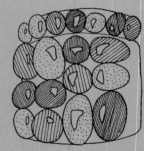

5 Work around the jar in the same way, rearranging the gems if necessary to make sure they fit together snugly.

6 Leave the jar to dry. It might take a couple of days, but be patient! It will be ready when the glue between the gems and the jar has become completely transparent.

7 Put down some more newspaper and put on some rubber gloves. With your fingers, rub the ready-mixed grout in the spaces between the gems.

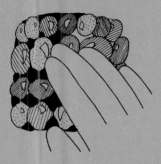

8 Wait about ten minutes and then use an old rag to wipe off any excess grout. If you rub off too much of the grout, just reapply it. Make sure the grout on top of the rim is smooth.

9 Leave to dry properly for a couple of days. Don't try and speed up the drying process by leaving the jar in a warm place as it will weaken the grout and make it crack and fall off.

TIP
Wipe any excess grout off your gloves before you wash them. If you have any grout left over in the pot, scrape it into the bin. Don't rinse large amounts of grout down the sink as you may block it up!

10 When the grout is dry, it is ready to paint. Using a small brush, paint one section at a time. If you accidentally paint over the gems, rub the paint off with a clean rag. Acrylic paint dries in a plastic-like layer, so it is possible to scratch it off with your fingernails if it has already dried, but don't leave it too long!

11 When the paint is dry, your night-light holder is ready to use. But pay attention to these tips for candle safety: always use a night-light rather than a normal candle; never leave any candle burning unattended; don't remove the night-light from the jar or try to re-light it if the wax is still liquid; and make sure a grown-up is around if you are using matches.

Cracker place cards

These cracker-shaped place cards decorated with shiny paper will make a stunning addition to the christmas dinner table.

YOU WILL NEED

- **A sheet of thin coloured card**
- **Coloured paper (plain and shiny)**
- **Star-shaped sequins**
- **Tracing paper**
- **Pencil**
- **Scissors**
- **Ruler**

1 Trace down the cracker template on p. 40 onto a piece of coloured card and cut out the main rectangle shape.

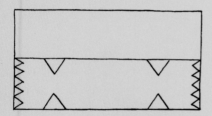

2 Score a line lengthways down the middle of the card as described on p. 8. Fold it in half with the drawing side facing outwards.

3 Now use a small pair of scissors to cut out the triangles to give the card its cracker shape. Cut through both sides of card at the same time.

4 Fold out the card so the cracker is flat. Decide which colours you want to use on your design and cut out the mosaic pieces. You will need roughly twenty 1 cm squares and lots of slightly smaller ones for the central frame.

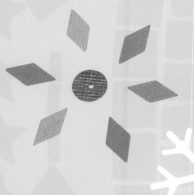

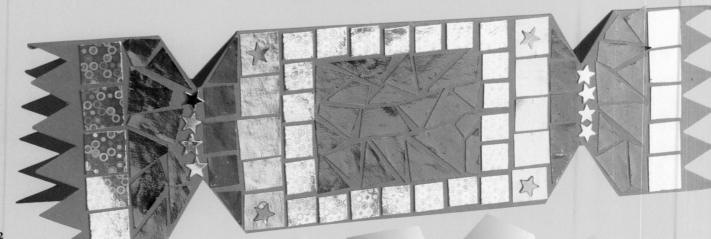

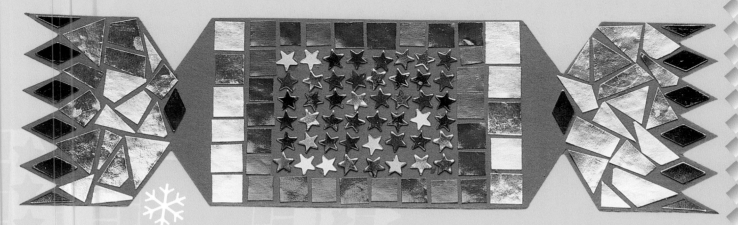

5 Stick five squares down each side of the cracker.

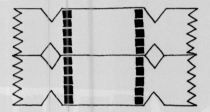

6 Make a frame inside these squares using the smaller squares.

7 Cut out a rectangle in plain, light-coloured paper to fit into the space left in the middle. The name is going here, so only do this on one side.

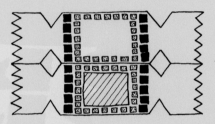

8 Fill in the middle space on the other side with your own design. You could fill it with sequins or stars, or a mosaic in shiny paper using squares or crazy paving.

9 Use a mixture of techniques and materials to fill in the ends of the cracker. As the card is coloured, you can also leave some areas blank.

Stained glass candle sticker

A mosaic of coloured cellophane on clear sticky-back plastic makes a beautiful stained glass effect candle that will light up a window when the sun shines in.

YOU WILL NEED

- **Coloured cellophane or cellophane sweet wrappers in orange, yellow, red and green**
- **Clear sticky-back plastic**
- **Masking tape**
- **Small scissors**
- **PVA glue and small plastic spreader**
- **Black washable felt-tip pen**

1 Trace or photocopy the candle template on p. 41 (enlarging it if you like). If you trace it, you will need to use a black felt-tip pen to go over the outline of the finished tracing so that the lines are really dark.

2 Stick the tracing or photocopy to your work surface with small pieces of masking tape.

3 Stick a sheet of clear sticky-back plastic over the candle drawing (paper side down, plastic side up) with more tape. The outline of the candle should still be visible through the sticky-back plastic.

4 Start your mosaic by doing the holly in the foreground. Cut a piece of green cellophane into random shapes no bigger than 3 x 1.5 cm.

5 Stick the cellophane pieces onto the plastic inside the holly outline starting at one side and working across. Don't worry if some pieces don't fit exactly into the outline, but make sure the holly doesn't lose its spiky look.

6 Now cut out some red squares for the candle. They should be big enough to fit three across the width of the candle.

7 Stick down the squares in three vertical rows, starting from the top of the candle. When you reach the holly, cut the squares to fit into the shape that's left.

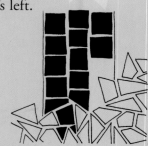

8 Cut out the shape of the centre of the flame in red and stick it down. For the outer part of the flame, cut orange cellophane into squares about 1 x 1 cm, then cut it to fit perfectly into the spaces left.

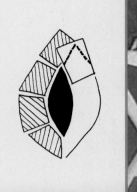

TIP

Get the shapes of the orange part of the flame exactly right by using this sneaky method! Lay a small piece of cellophane over the area you want to cover and draw the shape you need onto it with the felt-tip pen. Cut it out, wipe off any pen lines with a tissue and stick it into place.

9 Finish off your candle by cutting small random shapes from the yellow cellophane and stick them inside the circle of the candle's halo.

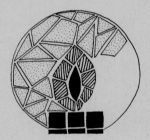

10 Leave the mosaic to dry flat, away from sunshine (keep it taped down if you can). The glue will take several days to dry as it is sandwiched between two layers of plastic. Wait until the candle looks transparent when you hold it up to the light.

11 When your mosaic has dried, peel the paper backing off another piece of clear sticky-back plastic and carefully stick it over the top of your design to protect the mosaic. Now cut round the outline of the whole design, peel off the paper on the back and stick it on a window.

Flying angel mobile

A trio of flying angels are suspended by silver thread to make this lovely mobile which sparkles as it moves.

YOU WILL NEED

- **A sheet of thin card about the size of this page**
- **A selection of shiny foil paper in different colours and/or shiny patterned gift wrap**
- **Leaf-shaped sequins**
- **Circular and star-shaped sequins**
- **Pale pink, orange and dark brown paper**
- **Tracing paper**
- **Pencil**
- **Scissors**
- **PVA glue and small plastic spreader**
- **Thick needle**
- **Fine silver thread**

1 Take the sheet of card and two pieces of foil paper that are roughly the same size. Stick the foil on each side of the card.

2 Trace down the angel template on p. 42 onto the card, and carefully cut it out. You will have a perfect angel shape that is shiny on both sides.

3 Cut strips of orange paper for the hair about 1.5 cm wide and then snip them into tiny strips.

4 Lay the strips around the top part of the head first, then do the rest of the hair in vertical lines. Work from the outside, doing one line on the left, then one on the right as you work inwards.

5 When you reach the centre, you might need to snip corners from the strips to make them fit.

6 Cut out a small triangle from the brown paper for the eye and stick it onto the angel's face. Fill in the rest of the face using pale pink pieces, cutting the pieces into shapes that fill the gaps.

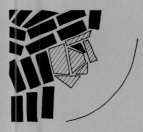

7 Make the angel's dress in a crazy paving style mosaic using either patterned gift wrap or foil paper. Decide on a design for a trim at the bottom of the sleeves and skirt. See the box for ideas or make up your own.

8 Cover the hands and the feet with pieces of pink using the same method as you did for the face.

9 Use some shiny gold paper to make the angel's halo. Cut a small square, slightly larger than the space between the edge of the angel's hair or face and the outline of the halo, then trim it to fit exactly. Repeat all the way round the halo.

TRIMS

Stars and circular sequins work well together, as small circles fit between the points of larger stars.

Stick two stars together to make a ten-pointed star, then stick a circular sequin on top. Repeat all the way along the row.

Lay a row of circular sequins, followed by a row of small paper strips, which are the same colour as the dress. Finish with stars and circles, as shown in example one.

10 Cover the wings with leaf-shaped sequins. If you can't find sequins, cut shapes from shiny paper. Lay them in rows, starting at the top, and turn them to follow the curve of the wing.

11 When one side is complete, turn the angel over and do the other side. You need three, or more, angels for the mobile.

12 Decide the angle you want your angel to hang by holding the top of the wing loosely between your thumb and forefinger. When you find an angle you like, pierce a hole in the place you were holding with a needle (ask a grown-up to help).

13 Do the same thing on the bottoms of the dresses for the top and middle angels.

14 Thread a long piece of silver thread through the hole of the angel you want at the top, and tie a knot in the loop next to the hole. Do the same with the other two angels using shorter lengths to connect them.

27

Christmas crowns

These dazzling crowns are better than anything you can find in a cracker. They will transform you into a king, queen or even the fairy on the top of the tree!

GOLD CROWN

YOU WILL NEED

- A sheet of thin gold card
- Small round sequins in white, green and gold
- Large round sequins in red and green
- Gold leaf-shaped sequins
- Shiny foil paper in red, green and holographic silver or gold
- Tracing paper
- Scissors
- Pencil
- Ruler
- PVA glue and small plastic spreader
- Sticky tape
- 4 pegs

1 Trace down crown template A on p. 43 onto the gold card, leaving a gap of at least 15 cm on either side of it.

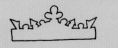

2 Continue the band of the crown on both sides using a ruler and pencil.

3 Cut out the crown carefully, using small pointed scissors. Then try it on, bending the bands around your head. Ask someone to make a pencil mark where they cross over.

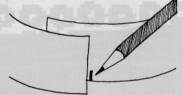

4 Extend the pencil mark to the top of the band, so you know where your design should finish.

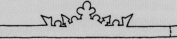

5 Start by doing the jewels in the centre of the crown. Cut out a small rectangle (1.5 x 2 cm) from the shiny green paper and snip each of the corners off. Stick it in the centre of the crown, then cut out some small squares from the holographic paper and stick them around it.

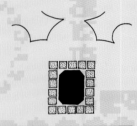

6 Stick a large circular green sequin directly above the central jewel, and then surround it with small white ones. Put a large red sequin above it, then finally arrange three gold leaves around the top.

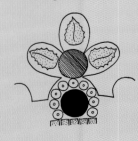

7 Stick a row of circular white sequins along the bottom of the crown, stopping at your pencil line on one side and continuing right to the end on the other side.

8 Stick a row of small green sequins on either side of the central jewel and continue the line round the rest of the rounded part of the crown and down on both sides.

9 Stick two large red sequins in the middle of the spaces that are left on each side and surround them with a circle of small gold sequins.

10 Decorate the remaining top parts of the crown with a mixture of holographic gold sequins and small diamonds in red and green.

11 Stick another row of circular white sequins along the top of the band. Cut out some squares from the red and green shiny paper and snip off the corners as in step 5. Alternate these along the band, separating each one with a line of small holographic squares.

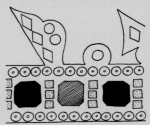

12 Stick the bands together at the back, overlapping the plain section with the decorated one. Leave it to dry for several hours, holding it together with four pegs, one on each corner of the stuck-down area. When it is dry, remove the pegs and stick a piece of sticky tape along the inside of the join for extra strength.

SNOW CROWN

YOU WILL NEED

- **A thin sheet of shiny blue card**
- **Large round silver sequins**
- **Small silver holographic sequins**
- **Silver snowflake sequins**
- **Diamond-shaped silver sequins**
- **Small white fluffy pompoms**
- **4 flat white buttons (2 cm diameter) – as sparkly as you can find!**
- **Small red plastic gem**
- **Basic equipment, as listed for the Gold Crown**

1 Trace down crown template B on p. 44 and draw, cut and measure it in the same way as described in steps 1-4 for the Gold Crown.

2 Stick a row of white fluffy pompoms along the bottom of the crown, leaving a small space between each one. If you can't find any pompoms, use white sequins instead.

3 Stick one of the buttons in the middle of the crown and surround it with holographic sequins. Stick the small red gem in the centre of the button.

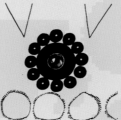

4 Working upwards on the central point, stick on another button, followed by a large silver circle, a silver snowflake and three diamonds on their points.

5 Stick a blue snowflake on top of each point of the crown. The tip of the point should go nearly all the way up the back of the snowflake so it is held on firmly.

6 Decorate the four other points with similar combinations of buttons and silver sequins. You don't need to cover all the blue foil with mosaic – it is pretty as it is!

7 Stick a silver snowflake onto the band next to the end points and then stick a few holographic circles at random over the rest of the band.

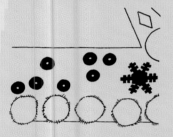

8 Assemble your crown as described in step 12 for the Gold Crown.

FAIRY CROWN

YOU WILL NEED

- **A thin sheet of white (or pale pink) card**
- **Silver and pink sequins in different shapes**
- **Basic equipment, as listed for the Gold Crown**

1 Trace down crown template B on p. 44 and draw, cut and measure it in the same way as described in steps 1-4 for the Gold Crown.

2 Stick a silver star on top of each point of the crown.

3 Stick a row of pink sequins along the bottom of the crown, and design a 'jewel' for the centre, then decorate with a wild mosaic of pink and silver sequins in your own design.

4 Assemble your crown as described in step 12 for the Gold Crown.

Furry reindeer mask

An unusual mosaic of fake fur and felt makes this reindeer mask look almost like the real thing!

YOU WILL NEED

- **A sheet of thin brown card**
- **Light brown (or grey) fake fur**
- **Dark brown (or dark grey) felt**
- **Pink felt**
- **Tracing paper**
- **Pencil**
- **Needlework scissors or craft knife**
- **Thick needle**
- **Thin dark brown elastic**

1 Trace down the reindeer mask template on p. 45 onto the brown card and carefully cut it out. Use a craft knife or needlework scissors to cut the eye holes as neatly as possible (ask a grown-up to help). Make sure the eye holes are the right width apart before you cut them out (see tip box).

2 Cut the fake fur into a strip about 3 cm wide and then snip it into random shapes.

3 Stick the fur pieces over the face part of the mask. Trim the pieces to fit into any small gaps.

TIP
To make sure the eye holes are in the right place for you, first trace out the mask (without the antlers) onto a scrap piece of paper. Cut out the eye holes and check that you can see through them. If you can't, decide how far apart the eyes need to be and re-draw them.

4 Cut two thin teardrop shapes about 2.5 cm long out of pink felt and stick one in the centre of each ear. Trim some small fur pieces to the correct shape and stick them around the pink felt to fill the rest of the ear.

TIP
See if you can find any off-cuts of fake fur in craft shops – you only need a little bit for your mask, so it will be much cheaper than buying a big piece.

5 Make the reindeer's antlers out of the dark brown felt, cutting each piece individually to fit the spaces. Start at the bottom and cut and stick each piece in whichever way seems to flow naturally. Snip tiny corners from each piece before you stick it down to give them a slightly rounded look. Use smaller pieces on the narrow areas and bigger pieces on the wider ones.

6 When your mosaic mask is complete, leave it to dry for an hour or so. Pierce a hole on each side of the mask with a thick needle (ask a grown-up to help you). Make sure the holes are not too close to the edge or going through any fur.

7 Stretch the piece of elastic round your head to work out how much you need. Don't make it too tight! Remember to allow a little extra to make knots. Cut it and thread it through the holes in the mask, then tie it with a knot at each side.

TIP
If the antlers are a bit floppy, glue two thin strips of card on the back of the mask to support them.

Three kings frieze

Use a variety of materials and techniques to make the three kings on their camels and a star for them to follow. Cut out and stick the shapes onto a wall to create a fabulous mosaic frieze.

YOU WILL NEED

- **A sheet of thin brown card**
- **A sheet of thin blue card**
- **Old glossy magazines**
- **Coloured paper in different shades of brown and flesh tones**
- **Multicoloured sequins in different shapes**
- **Small plastic gems (optional)**
- **Plain and holographic shiny paper**
- **Scissors**
- **Hole puncher (optional)**
- **PVA glue and small plastic spreader**
- **Tracing paper**
- **Black or brown felt-tip pen**
- **Craft knife**
- **Blue-tac**

1 Photocopy and enlarge the king templates on p. 46-48. Cut them out and draw round them, or trace the outline of each king onto a piece of brown card.

2 Start with the king's crown and head. Use a mixture of gold paper and sequins to fill in the shape of the crown.

3 Trace the shape of the king's face onto a piece of flesh tone paper, cut it out and stick it down. Draw on an eye with the felt-tip pen. Do the same for the shape of the hand.

4 Do the hair and beard in the same way as the angel's on p. 26 with strips cut from glossy magazines, or use ripped pieces of coloured paper (see step 9 for how to do this).

5 Fill in the king's robe using any style of mosaic you like. Do the sleeves first, following the lines on the drawing, so that they stand out from the rest of the robe. Cut shapes for the shoes out of different coloured paper.

TIP
Whatever style of mosaic you choose – squares or crazy paving – mix in the odd sequin to make the mosaic sparkle.

6 Choose a different mosaic technique to do the saddle. Create a stripy pattern by mixing alternate lines of shapes and colours, or make plain pieces look more interesting by sticking sequins on the top. See the box for different suggestions of how to create an exotic fringing on the saddle.

7 Choose another style of mosaic for the camel blanket. Try using a hole puncher to make little circles out of patterns from magazines and arrange them in rows, working from the outside and moving in.

8 When the saddle area is complete, move onto the bridle, using whatever mosaic style you like (circles, strips or squares). Add some simple fringing from one of the ideas in the box. Make the reins using thin strips of paper.

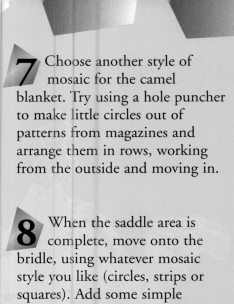

FRINGING

LEAVES AND CIRCLES
Lay a row of leaves, pointing downwards, then lay circles above the bases of the leaves. Now lay another row of leaves and circles, making sure the circles fit into the spaces between the points of the leaves.

STARS AND MOONS
Arrange a line of crescent moon shapes all facing the same way under a line of stars

DIAMONDS
Use a single line of diamonds for a bridle and a thicker layer for the saddle. Make patterns by varying the colours.

CIRCLES
Circles arranged in single or double rows on the bridle look just like the brightly coloured pompoms that decorate camels today. Use sequins, tiny plastic gems, or a mixture of both.

10 Stick the pieces onto the camel, starting at one end and moving across. Adjust the size of the pieces for the legs and tail so that they fit the width perfectly.

9 Use a mosaic of ripped paper shapes to make the camel's body. Rip strips, roughly 1 cm wide, from one of the sheets of brown paper and then tear them into small pieces.

11 Tear out shapes in dark brown for the camel's eye, nostril and the end of its tail. Rip out a shape for the eyelid in a brown which is lighter than the body colour. You can use a different brown for each camel or make them all the same.

12 When the camels are finished, cut them out carefully, leaving a small gap around the edge of the mosaic pieces. Use a craft knife to cut out the space underneath the reins (ask a grown-up to help).

13 Trace down the star template on p. 38 onto the blue card and cover with a crazy-paving mosaic of silver and silver holographic paper (and the odd silver star if you like). Cut it out in the same way as you did for the kings.

14 Arrange the kings in a line with the star above them and stick them to a wall with Blu-tac.

AMAZING CHRISTMAS MOSAICS:
SNOWFLAKE & STAR TEMPLATES

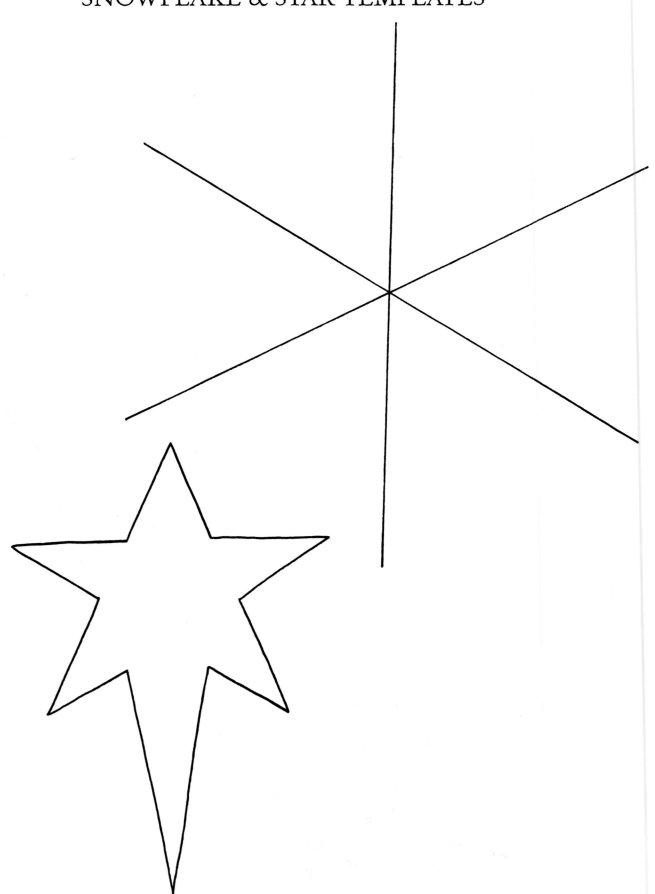

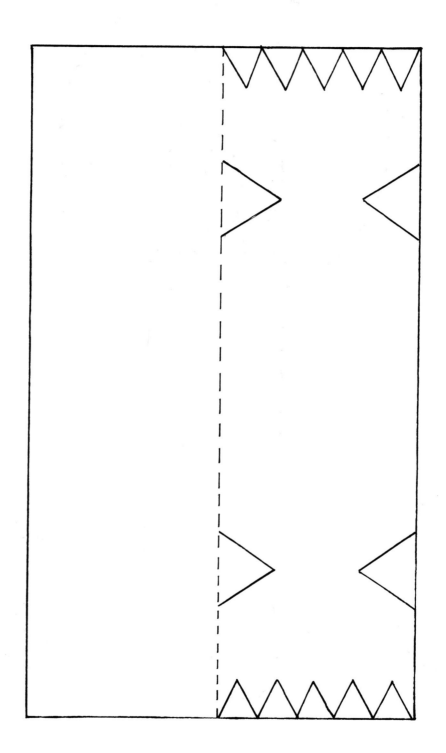

AMAZING CHRISTMAS MOSAICS: CROWN TEMPLATE A

AMAZING CHRISTMAS MOSAICS: CROWN TEMPLATE B

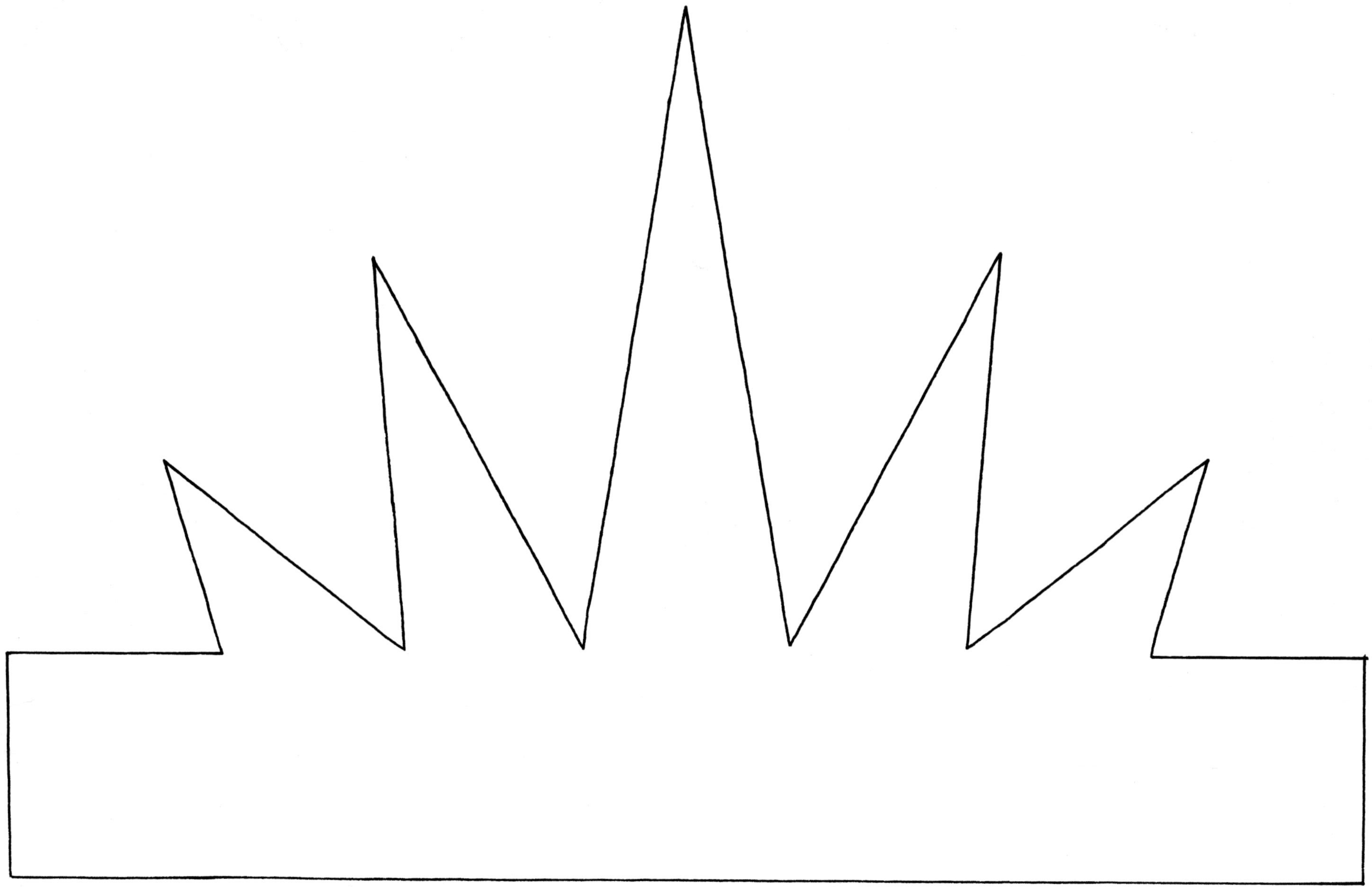

AMAZING
CHRISTMAS
MOSAICS:
REINDEER MASK
TEMPLATE